BEYOND THESE THINGS

Mary Martina Dockter

ISBN 979-8-9907297-1-1 (paperback)
ISBN 979-8-9907297-0-4 (eBook)

Copyright © 2024 by Mary Martina Dockter

All rights reserved. No part of this publication may be reproduced, distributed, or transmitted in any form or by any means, including photocopying, recording, or other electronic or mechanical methods without the prior written permission of the publisher.

Printed in the United States of America

DEDICATED TO MY FATHER, NICK
MY MOTHER, RUTH AND STEPMOTHER, ROSE
THANK YOU FOR YOUR GUIDANCE

CONTENTS

BEYOND THESE THINGS 1
BEAUTY BEYOND 2
LIFE'S LESSONS 3
COME WHAT MAY 4
THE HIGH WAY 5
THE LONG RUN 6
LUCKY ONE 7
NOTHING FOR GRANTED 8
DEAD SPACE 9
A SIMPLE LIFE 10
BE ME 11
I AM ME 12
RELATIVITY 13
PROCUL HARUN 14
THE AIR SHARES 15
YOUNG AT HEART 16
EYES OF STEALTH 17
BE THE ROCK 18
A FATHER'S LOVE 19
MY DAD 20
A GOOD MAN 21
MOTHER 22
A MOTHER'S PRAYER 23
TO MY CHILDREN 24
TO BE A HERO 25
LIFT THEM UP 26
KIDS AND KATS 27
REVOLUTION 28

FAMILIES ARE FOREVER	29
A GOOD PERSON	30
HOME IS NEAR	31
HOME IS WITHIN	32
HOMEBOUND	33
HOME IS HERE	34
THE ELYSIAN FIELDS	35
UP YONDER	36
LIFE GOES ON	37
FORGIVENESS	38
AIM HIGH	39
I BELIEVE	40
DIVINE DIRECTION	41
GOD'S NEAR	42
GOD'S GIFT	43
VOICE OF REASON	44
IN SEASON	45
AUTUMN GOLD	46
STAY GOLD	47
HARMONY	48
THEY'RE THERE	49
AN EAR FULL	50
DREAM DRIVEN	51
SEARCH WITHIN	52
UPLIFTING	53
LIFE	54
LIVE LIFE	55
BETTER BE	56
CHOOSE WISELY	57
SPOTLESS ADVICE	58
WOE IS WE	59
DECLUTTER	60
JUST BE HAPPY	61

LESS IS MORE	62
UNWRAP HAPPINESS	63
SMILE AWHILE	64
SMALL THINGS	65
MINUTIA	66
DAISY DAYS	67
IN TUNE	68
ONE'S COCOON	69
BUTTERFLY WINGS	70
LOVE	71
NOWHERE	72
NOWHERE I'D RATHER BE	73
CLIMBING TREE	74
ROOTED	75
UP ON A TREE TOP	76
UP HIGH ON A SWING	77
IF I COULD FLY	78
BE THE KITE	79
FLIGHT OF A KITE	80
KITE HEIGHT	81
RUN WITH THE WIND	82
WIND ON MY FACE	83
WHIMSICAL WIND	84
IN THE AIR	85
WHISPERING WIND	86
BE THERE	87
BE LIKE THE TURTLE	88
LET LADYBUGS COME	89
HUMMINGBIRD	90
BE NOW	91
BE STILL	92
JUST A ROCK'N	93
TAKE IT EASY	94

LIFE IS A HOOT	95
LIFE WILL BE	96
BREEZE ON BY	97
JUMP	98
TAKE A CHANCE	99
BEYOND THE SIDEWALK	100
CHERISH CHILDHOOD	101
PETER PAN PHILOSOPHY	102
JUST A DREAM	103
LULLABY SEA	104
TAKE ME BACK	105
CHILDHOOD DAYS	106
HALCYON DAYS	107
GO BEYOND	108
MY HAPPY PLACE	109
NOTHING COMPARES	110
THE BEST DAY	111
SO PEACEFUL	112
PEACEFUL PLACES	113
MY PERFECT PLACE	114
KALEIDOSCOPE	115
BE THE BALLOON	116
LET GO	117
GO WITH THE FLOW	118
JUST FLOAT	119
LET IT GO	120
WHATEVER	121
LONG GONE	122
HARD KNOCKS	123
FUNDAMENTAL	124
ACTUAL FACTUAL	125
THE CLOUD	126
CHOOSE WISELY	127

LIFE IS MESSY	128
FRIENDLY FIRE	129
DECEPTION	130
WHAT THE	131
A SILENT VOICE	132
DUPLICITY	133
EVENTUALLY	134
RIDE THE STORM	135
BULLY ADVICE	136
THE BLIND HORSE	137
BEING THERE	138
SALTY ADVICE	139
RAMBLING ROAD	140
WAYWARD ONE	141
OFF THE BEATEN TRACK	142
WHAT MAY BE	143
WATCH OUT	144
PASSING BY	145
SHOOTING STAR	146
QUASAR	147
MAGNETAR	148
RADIANT	149
RING SHINE	150
JUST BE	151
UNIQUELY YOU	152
ODDITIES	153
ROGUE WAYS	154
ROAM FREE	155
LIVING BREATHING	156
FRAGILE THINGS	157
ABOVE ALL ELSE	158
MY LIFE MATTERS	159
WHAT MATTERS	160

LOVE MATTERS MOST	161
WHAT MATTERS MOST	162
NOTHING ELSE MATTERS	163
LIVING FOR ME	164
RECKONING	165
HOLDS WATER	166
REVISED	167
HOLDS MORE WATER	168
RIDDANCE	169
TRUTH BE TOLD	170
SOMETHING ELSE	171
GRAYISH	172
SHADES OF GRAYS	173
LOCH NESS GUESS	174
BALLAD OF BIGFOOT	175
MYSTICAL BIGFOOT	176
NOBODY CARES	177
WITHIN	178
COMING AND GOING	179
LET IT JUST BE	180
THE CHANGE	181
GROWING OLD IS NOT FOR SISSIES	182
IMPRISONED IN TIME	183
SEQUENT	184
HOME SWEET HOME	185
BREVITY	186
BEYOND THE STARS	187
INEVITABLE	188

BEYOND THESE THINGS

Life is what you make of it, no matter what
No one can take from it unless you let it but
There's times, when it is out of your control

And for whatever reason not the one to stroll
The lessons in life the one's before you bring
When it's taught by them beyond these things

2023

BEAUTY BEYOND

Open your closed eyes, and see what is around you.
The wonderment of the earth is a masterpiece anew.
Just waiting to be explored the mountains to the sea.
There is so much to discover there is so much to see.
Take the time experience the gift before you're gone.
For this world is our blessing with its beauty beyond.

2023

LIFE'S LESSONS

Within oneself there is a silent voice.
That, one hears, when given a choice.
So live your life by not guessing then.
And learn from others in life's lessons.

2022

COME WHAT MAY

No one can predict the future beyond.
We live our lives nothing goes wrong.
Not thinking the day could be our last.
Yesterday's forgotten they're the past.

Maybe it is good that we live this way.
Why worry by saying come what may.
No one can predict the future beyond.
We live our lives nothing goes wrong.

2023

THE HIGH WAY

On the road thru life there are many paths.

Where, one is safe and the other a bypath.

You can take one, for the fun, of a joyride.

Where, chances of an accident, will abide.

Or do you take a slower way and be good.

Where it might be less traveled but would.

Be safer in the long run when on the road.

Where, life has many paths along its way.

For, there is a wrong way or the high way.

2023

THE LONG RUN

Life is a race and the finish line is death.
In a marathon that will end out of breath.
It doesn't matter if the road taken up hill.
Or path that's level eventually it will still.
Lead all to the same place where it's done.
As your living life racing for the long run.

2023

LUCKY ONE

There once was a man who had riches galore
But did little to enrich his life, or others more
He spent his time within the walls of its stone
Worried his estate taken, he never would roam
And died alone with all the money in the world
Forsaken and forgotten lying in a casket burled

There once was a man who had no riches at all
But that didn't stop to enrich him or others call
He spent his time helping those without a home
Worried their peace of mind taken it was known
And died the richest man for all that he has done
Never forgotten or forsaken, he is, the lucky one

2023

NOTHING FOR GRANTED

Take nothing for granted on the highway of life.
One may be riding in luxury, or thumbing strife.
Either way the journey's the same where we go.
As we'll meet at the road's end then we'll know.
The baggage we carried doesn't mean anything.
Everything accumulated here, we cannot bring.
So lighten your load, and live life with a smile.
Take nothing for granted to be thankful awhile.

2023

DEAD SPACE

There are no luggage racks on a hearse
You can't take it with you is the curse
Many have tried to pay with their purse
But in the end has made matters worse
There are no luggage racks on a hearse

Here within we eventually have to face
The coldness and darkness of this place
With no where to go, there is no haste
When one finds they lie in dead space
Here within we eventually have to face

There are no luggage racks on a hearse
You can't take it with you is the curse
Many have tried to pay with their purse
But in the end has made matters worse
There are no luggage racks on a hearse

2008

A SIMPLE LIFE

When I was young I learned a valuable lesson in life.
I'd play outdoors in the woods is forgetting all strife.
The grass is under your feet, and dirt is on your face.
With the wind at your back as there is no other place.
I would rather be for its where one can truly be alive.
And to this day, I'll reminisce, by living a simple life.

2023

BE ME

There is no one else I would rather be.

Than just myself and to just be me.

2023

I AM ME

I am me.
I am different as,
Inert air from a breeze,
A river from a sea,
An ocean from a shore.
As I breathe,
Inert air instills entity,
Self-contained existence.
My river flows from the torpid land,
To an island beset by sea.
The ocean of my soul,
Besiege the shore by undertow.
As I breathe,
The inert air of others will blow,
Intertwined we become a breeze.
My river flows into the sea of mankind,
Intertwined we nourish each other.
The ocean of my soul,
Intertwined will touch distant shores.
As I breathe,
The inert air blows to a breeze,
The river flows into a sea,
An ocean must touch a shore.
Although I am different,
I am interchangeable.
I am me.

1974

RELATIVITY

It's all relative what you make of it.
Good or bad what one takes from it.
Lessons learned are different maybe.
There are many opinions of truth be.
Out in the universe someone's mind.
Who to say I'm right, yours or mine.
Just be careful which side you're on.
The wrong one your freedom's gone.
It's all relative what you make of it.
Good or bad what one takes from it.

2023

PROCUL HARUN

Far beyond these things is another universe
It is a vast world where all minds' converse
No need to speak in words but with thought
We'll be connected to each other in this plot

Liken oceans on earth as well in outer space
For, the "Man in the Moon" a forgotten face
When on this planet mankind dies at the end
But, far beyond these things, new life begins

2023

THE AIR SHARES

A gift to us all the minute we are born.

For, life takes its first breath before clothes are worn.

2022

YOUNG AT HEART

Days go by faster than one can count.
Before you know it, time's in amount.
Larger than one wishes the number be.
Wasn't it yesterday you were just tiny.
And playing games and joking around.
Being free, living life a way it's bound.
Its freedom of youth not meant to part.
If one lives their life, be young at heart.

2021

EYES OF STEALTH

Behind their heads, is hidden from sight
As a child believes no one sees so might
Be able to get away actions done wrong
When a parent's out of sight and is gone

But, to their surprise it is already known
That's not possible for nothing is shown
And the child believes it's magic instead
A parent's eyes on the back of their head

2023

BE THE ROCK

Be the one who is strong.
Be the one hatred's gone.
Be the one carries a load.
Be the one a path showed.

Be the one beacon's light.
Be the one who does right.
Be the one they may mock.
Be the one the mighty rock.

2023

A FATHER'S LOVE

It's stronger than the strongest bond
That holds together, never broken gone

Deeper than the deepest, blue sea
That swims aquatic life, living free

Higher than the highest mount
That touches the wondrous sky no doubt

Brighter than the brightest, twinkling star
That shines each night from afar

And wider than the longest arms spread apart
That is how much a father's love is in your heart

2019

MY DAD

Before I was born
His story was there
About a brave, young man
I wish to share

The years of his youth
In lessons he found
Were not from a book
But, from his small town

And the guidance he knew
From his parents' strong
Even when he's away to war
Back home is where he belongs

With the love of his life
And their children four
He works hard for them all
That's what a father is for

Before I was born
His story I am so glad
About a brave, young man
I'm proud to call my dad

2023

A GOOD MAN

Puts family first

Selfishness hurts

His loving heart

Won't depart

A ring on hand

Trust demands

And vows to talk

Will never walk

2012

MOTHER

Mother another word for love
Who, is sent from above
And is blest by celestial grace
For, she will take God's place
While here on earth, heaven's way
Together again someday
Mother another word for love

Mother another word for hope
So her family may cope
When she has been released
To be with God's eternal peace
For her life will always stay
Within our hearts we pray
Mother another word for hope

2022

A MOTHER'S PRAYER

From the time a child is born.
And long to when they're grown.
A mother will keep you warm.
Within her heart you'll be known.
For God will hear her prayers.
The many blessings she will say.
I will place them in your care.
So please look after them today.
By, granting me the guidance.
As I protect them in your place.
I pray I'm blest with patience.
And love for them upon my face.

2020

TO MY CHILDREN

(Bo, Brittney and Ty)
Since the hour of your birth
My heart pulsates beyond mirth
Unselfishness, a mother's revealment
For my children are my true fulfillment
Paternal gifts' bequest, by passion above
You are forever blessed by maternal love
Rock back and forth within loving arms
This day forward sheltered from harm

2004

TO BE A HERO

A little boy sat with his daddy on his knee.
And, together they sat watching their T.V.
Some time had passed by without a sound.
When, suddenly his son had turned around.
"Why do you like watching sports so much?
Are they like a hero to look up to as such?"
His father couldn't believe words in his ear.
It troubled him so and brought him to tears.
He held his son tight, quietly telling him no.
"They're not to look up to watching them go.
They may be fast, hard workers for the team.
But their appearance son is not what it seems.
To be a hero one does not know that they are.
Those on T.V. think they already are a star."
He pointed to the kitchen as his wife was near.
Washing supper dishes as a table was cleared.
"Do you see your mom working hard for us all?
She is our silent hero for she has taken the call.
For, a mother is there when all others are not.
She cares about a son while players are bought."
A little boy climbed down off his daddy's knee.
He ran into the kitchen so his mother could see.
And he wrapped his arms tight around her waist.
With tears in his eyes words came without haste.
"I love you mommy," as he drew her in near, so.
To then whisper in her ear, "You are my hero."

2009

LIFT THEM UP

As you look down at your children at your feet.
Wide eyed and trusting arms, reach out to greet.
For you're the only one, they truly depend upon.
A mother or father is the heart, a future beyond.
Let not a day go by, this precious gift unopened.
Your love must always be there, they are hoping.
Security reaches out to them when they are pups.
So with caring eyes and loving arms lift them up.

2012

KIDS AND KATS

So you think you're the boss, the big cheese.
The owner of a cat or a parent that over sees.
For, the joke is on you, if you think that way.
Because cats and kids have the one final say.
Oh they let you believe that you're in charge.
With their cute faces, and eyes that are large.
But in the end we know the truth will be told.
So if you want to be the boss a puppy is sold.

2012

REVOLUTION

When you were so young
Lying in the warm crib asleep
I dreamt of your future begun
Older as my heart seeks

Now, you think yourself old
So acrimonious, my heart weeps
I look back when you did as told
Lying in the warm crib asleep

2004

FAMILIES ARE FOREVER

Families are forever
As memories to be treasured
For nothing can be measured
The love from each member
So no matter just remember
Families are forever

2011

A GOOD PERSON

My wish for my children is this.
You may think, it is one of bliss.
It's more than riches to be found.
And a life with treasures abound.
There is more to life, in only this.
A good person must be on the list.

2023

HOME IS NEAR

Where ever you go home is here.
Within your heart, home is near!

2023

HOME IS WITHIN

Home is within
For there you begin
To know one self
The love for yourself
A place in the heart
Forever never part
For there one begins
Home is within

2011

HOMEBOUND

There's no place like home when not at home
The different places and faces when you roam
Can never replace those loved ones left behind
And even though separated stay on one's mind
For the journey back, as sweet as honey found
When, there's no place like home, homebound

2023

HOME IS HERE

Where ever you go, there is your home.

No matter how far or near you may roam.

For home is where one puts down roots.

As you settle within by resting your boots.

To make where ever you go so very dear.

And no matter where you are home is here.

2023

THE ELYSIAN FIELDS

Do you sometimes look up into the sky and wonder?
Is there a place beyond this one here way up yonder?
Is this as good as it gets, this world we live on earth?
Is the life we have now, the only one since our birth?
Is death an end of our existence blowing in the wind?
Is dying a door to enter heaven a new life will begin?
Is there a place beyond this one here way up yonder?
Do you sometimes look up into the sky and wonder?

2023

UP YONDER

Sometimes I wish to ponder
        What, is beyond up yonder
Beyond the mountains high
        Way up high above the sky
Where blue turns to a black
        And night and day are exact
Just to float without a care
        While you're going nowhere
But to look down from afar
        As planet Earth is like a star
Sometimes I wish to ponder
        What, is beyond up yonder

2021

LIFE GOES ON

Life goes on

From here to beyond

In its time

All will be fine

When mistakes are made

Forgiveness saves

So from here to beyond

Life goes on

2012

FORGIVENESS

There is one undeniable truth to heal wounds afflicted.
Bare the venom of sin our fathers' inherited addicted.
Open the hearts of many by extending hands of mercy.
Hoping an out stretched hand seeks others mirthfully.
To look beyond our differences to see we are the same.
You and I the world's problem and we are all to blame.
Be the solution, the destruction of hatred in willingness.
We are amid angels to look upon man with forgiveness.

2004

AIM HIGH

Aim for heaven,

And all things on earth are possible!

2020

I BELIEVE

I BELIEVE
A new day begins, the morning sun rises.
The gift of life wins when our spirit arises.
And we breathe essence of all that is great.
With so many presents when we're awake.

I BELIEVE
The glistening dew kisses a radiant flower.
As honey bees flew pollinating by the hour.
For the petals decorate land with every hue.
A blanket of color began, timeless and new.

I BELIEVE
All God's creatures walk, and fly on earth.
They have so many features different births.
It's an imagination beyond, wildest dreams.
This world we belong, this wondrous thing.

I BELIEVE
Mankind is to rule taking care of this place.
But we are here to be a tool, to be His face.
A new day begins as the morning sun rises.
I do believe in Him my grateful heart arises.

2019

DIVINE DIRECTION

Worry never wins
When prayer begins

2018

GOD'S NEAR

Every time I see blue skies above,
I see a blanket in clouds of His love.

Every time I see majestic mountains high,
I see a reminder He is always nearby.

Every time I see the green grass and trees,
I see a symbol to why we fall to our knees.

Every time I see the vast oceans of blue,
I see a vision of many blessings from you.

Every time I see the rippling rivers flow,
I see the abundant gifts we've come to know.

Every time I see a precious baby lie,
I see a sign of His power the reason why.

Every time I see family and friends dear,
I see His mirror image for God is near.

2019

GOD'S GIFT

The most wondrous gift God gave to man.
It's not a gift one is able to hold in a hand.
Nor pick it up to rip open wrapping paper.
Even though, it is decorated, by His labor.

For, He has given us the waves of the seas.
And birds in the air that dance on a breeze.
And a forest green with its bounty of trees.
So I thank God for His gift, for all of these.

2021

VOICE OF REASON

Bees have hives, trees have leaves
No one can deny the truth of these

Water is wet, the planets are round
It wasn't long ago a science found

We breathe the air, oxygen's made
In return we exhale dioxide to aid

The grass is green, the sky so blue
A voice of reason life's many hues

2023

IN SEASON

All in season
>Four, a reason

A winter's chill
>If weak it kills

A spring's thaw
>Life may crawl

A summer's light
>Beauty's might

An autumn's weep
>Death to creep

All in season
>Four, a reason

2023

AUTUMN GOLD

Bright colored hues do magically adorn them.
When leaves in the trees become nature's gems.
As they blow in the wind with shimmer of light.
They are jewels of the changing landscape sight.
This blessed treasured season is for all to behold.
For, we're enriched with beauty in autumn gold.

2012

STAY GOLD

Rise, the morning sun to greet the day
With its amber rays, and glow, so bold
If only, our life's direction would obey
And be as the rising sun and stay gold

Shy, the radiant gaze a sunflower shows
With its au rum petals play a sun's hold
If only, our life's direction would know
And be as all sunflowers and stay gold

Lies, the setting sun that ends each day
With its auburn rays, and glow, so bold
If only, our life's direction would obey
And be as the setting sun and stay gold

2008

HARMONY

All in order, rest assured

Life will follow His direction

Do not worry, blest assured

Like the flower we are perfection

2010

THEY'RE THERE

Oh you may think it is only clouds that you see

When staring up at heaven in nothing to believe

But the eyes will deceive and play tricks on you

For they're there all around if only we do choose

To look beyond, there is more than clouds to see

When staring up at heaven, angels we do believe

2022

AN EAR FULL

Dreams are angels,
Whispering in your ears,
Never stop listening,
Always keep believing!

2020

DREAM DRIVEN

Awake to a purpose in life's vision

For life is a journey with a mission

Mere dreams to fulfill of one self

Naught meant to be left on the shelf

For one's thoughts one has wished

Are there to be checked off one's list

2005

SEARCH WITHIN

No need, to go outside of your realm.
When, deep inside you may find them.
It is there you will feel strength to fly.
And live out your dreams if only to try.

For therein oneself is the key to unlock.
The very essence others do try to block.
So take courage to discover your perch.
By looking within instead as you search.

2023

UPLIFTING

Look around you and what do you see.
There is so much beauty in the world to believe.
In yourself and others within one's soul.
For we are meant for the good in life is our goal.

And the air we breathe the breath to begin.
We live each day with gratitude and love so then.
Humanity will take care of glorious things.
There is much beauty in the world, it is uplifting.

2022

LIFE

Living

Is

For

Everyone

2005

LIVE LIFE

Wake up in the morning and take a deep breath.
A new day's risen, with opportunities in depth.
Shake off daunted dust from yesterday's yawn.

For today is a fresh way for worries to be gone.
So believe in your heart, life is more than strife.
It's the most wonderful gift, if you just live life.

2023

BETTER BE

Better to be safe than sorry be on guard.
When, going through life living at large.
There may be good times looking ahead.
But, there could be trouble times instead.
So be prepared for whatever you and me.
And take nothing for granted better to be.

2023

CHOOSE WISELY

The choices made today,

Will pave your future's way!

2011

SPOTLESS ADVICE

Make your bed
Clears your head

Declutter stash
Eliminates trash

Vacuum bound
Cleans all around

Dishes put away
Is a happy day

Make your bed
Clears your head

2018

WOE IS WE

Every one has their woes

That's just the way it goes

For no one ever knows

What the future shows

2012

DECLUTTER

You're in the gutter,
When your mind is filled with clutter,
Stop collecting negative thoughts,
By being a hoarder.

Start having positive thoughts,
By being a sorter,
You can discern one from the other,
It's time to be happy so just declutter.

2011

JUST BE HAPPY

Of all the wishes I could wish for you.
There's one above all I wish to be true.
It's not my wish for you to have wealth.
But this wish, it is good for your health.
And help you along if woes come to be.
My one wish for you is to just be happy.

2023

LESS IS MORE

Less Ignorance

Less Helplessness

Less Poverty

Less Hunger

Less Jealousy

Less Envy

Less Worry

Less Sickness

Less Evil

Less Violence

Less Hatred

Less War

2012

UNWRAP HAPPINESS

Of all the gifts, one may find under the Christmas tree.
Or a birthday party, with friends, celebrating with glee.
A present so special it is a gift to oneself from the heart.
But is shared to all others for its pleasure will not depart.
It puts a smile on your face, for it is the gift of true bliss.
When, one opens this bequest by unwrapping happiness.

2023

SMILE AWHILE

It doesn't take much to put one of these on.
When it's already there and ready to belong.
Be apart of your face as you face life's woes.
Better to be happy than sad one should know.
It doesn't take much you should try it awhile.
Tum a frown upside down to make it a smile.

2023

SMALL THINGS

It is the small things in life that matter.
For, they're the ones that won't shatter.

A field of wild flowers a smell as sweet.
Like expensive perfume in stores to seek.

The colors of autumn leaves, paint a sky.
Like museum of art displayed to the eye.

Sparkling stars decorate the dark of night.
Like diamonds worn as jewelry's delight.

A brisk walk in nature, wind in your hair.
Like driving a convertible going nowhere.

It is the small things in life that do matter.
For, they're the ones that will, not shatter.

2023

MINUTIA

In all greatness, there is smallness.
It is the foundation to being grand.
From the beginning we're all blest.
Like the minute granule in the land.

With a drop of rain there's a notion.
As rivers flow they're able to reach.
Join together, and will fill the ocean.
So with sand may become the beach.

For then a blade of grass will grow.
Like a lone tree in a field has stood.
As grass soon becomes the meadow.
The forest will be acreages of wood.

And cells in living organisms accrue.
In the beginning, there will be, man.
But with each person humanity grew.
Its little things in life that's so grand.

2011

DAISY DAYS

May your day be like a flower!
Joyfully dancing in sunshine,
Boyishly standing in the rain,
Playfully blowing in the wind,
Magically growing in a Daisy,
In the garden of everyday life!

2012

IN TUNE

Listen to the music, playing all around.

For the earth sings a song I have found.

The wind blows its melody in a cocoon.

It keeps the musical instruments in tune.

One must quiet the mind and be at ease.

To hear its magic our planet is of peace.

2022

ONE'S COCOON

Within your soul a chrysalis forms.

It's there taking shape before you're born.

When, each person to be begins to grow.

There's a positive outlook or a negative low.

So will you spread your wings in life to fly?

Or lay dormant and afraid until you die.

For the soul is the key to all in bloom.

Is there a beautiful butterfly in your cocoon?

2012

BUTTERFLY WINGS

Of all the flying things that, I see.
There is one, of majestic delicacy.
It dances in the air as if in a ballet.
But quietly sits on a flower to stay.
For just a little while then it flings.
Like an angel with butterfly wings.

2023

LOVE

Love is a butterfly.

Her tender

wings ache with each

caress of velvet.

Fluttering

to the heavens.

1974

NOWHERE

Nowhere, I'd rather be, than right here.
Not, in the past, or in the future is clear.
For I know exactly this moment in time.
Who I am and what I stand for I am fine.
The world may be chaotic but no not me.
I have peace of Jesus Christ so I am free.

2023

NOWHERE I'D RATHER BE

Of all the places, I have seen.
There are few that I do dream.
And wish to revisit in the past.
To make memories that'll last.

But there is one comes to mind.
Every time I'm there, I do find.
For, I'm within a realm of trees.
There, is nowhere, I'd rather be.

2022

CLIMBING TREE

Of all the trees you see in the forest around.
There's but a few good for climb I've found.
Some are too short, and not worth your time.
While others are too tall and a fall is a crime.
The best would be straight, liken a ruler stick.
And branches used as steps on a ladder quick.
To get to the top so to take in all that you see.
When finding the right one, for climbing tree.

2022

ROOTED

Deep within one's being is a majestic tree.
It's where we branch out and become free.
Steadfast in the beliefs we come to believe.
They're our core values no one can deceive.
And take away what is rooted in one's soul.
By chopping to stop and try to take control.

2022

UP ON A TREE TOP

On top of the world there you will find.
As you climb up a tree there to unwind.
Not a care is there will bring you down.
Not even hustle and bustle that's around.
For the best place to be, a peaceful prop.
When, high in the clouds up on a tree top.

2022

UP HIGH ON A SWING

The perfect tree for a swing has a branch straight and long.
And tall enough so rope can dangle close to the dirt strong.
So holes can be drilled on a wooden plank made for a seat.
It's the right size for a child to sit in wonder, a sky to meet.
All is needed a push strong enough to touch clouds to bring.
Such joy for an explorer this exhilaration up high on a swing.

2022

IF I COULD FLY

If I could fly, I think I would like to be

An eagle of radiant beauty and majesty

With wings that spread across this land

And glide on air in a commanding stand

My eyes like sharpen knives will pierce

In the sky I'll capture prey as I'm fierce

But alone, my flight of silence does cry

I am an eagle yes an eagle, if I could fly

2021

BE THE KITE

Maybe, just maybe we are granted a wish.
If we imagine in ourselves what we insist.
I wish to be free as a bird without feathers.
Be the color of a rainbow without weather.
To glide on the wind that carries you along.
But strong enough to land the wind is gone.
I'll dance in the air with the help one's care.
Joy will be my delight, I be the kite to share.

2022

FLIGHT OF A KITE

Hold on, tiny fingers, to this delight.
Don't let go it might go out of sight.
It flies in the air with it your dreams.
And it floats without a care it seems.

Dancing through the clouds it plays.
With a tug or with a release it obeys.
As the string, gives it life in a breeze.
Then be captured in branches of trees.

And it floats without a care it seems.
It flies in the air with it your dreams.
Don't let go, it might go out of sight.
Hold on, tiny fingers, to this, delight.

2022

KITE HEIGHT

If I could, I'd imagine myself being a kite.
When, a tiny hand can no longer hold tight.
A string is keeping me from flying up high.
But now I'm free, I'm able to touch the sky.
And soar above clouds, hoping I just might.
Be like an eagle in flight, by my kite height.

2022

RUN WITH THE WIND

Spread the arms like wings of a bird.
And close your eyes not saying a word.
Feel the gentle wind within your hair.
It caresses your face nothing compares.
Then run with the wind to reach a height.
As you pretend to soar, and take flight.

2021

WIND ON MY FACE

Nothing will compare to a brisk walk.
It's in nature where the breeze can talk.
And I hear the voice of a mother's grace.
When, I explore with the wind on my face.

2022

WHIMSICAL WIND

Let's play outside and see what is there.
Maybe we'll discover a friend in the air.
It's one that comes and goes as it please.
And, even when it is there, not one sees.

This friend nearby, will be by your side.
A brisk walk in the forest, it will, abide.
When, trees wave, hello, with the leaves.
As they, are thankful for the cool breeze.

A sauntering brook's also taking a stroll.
For both of you are adrift along the knoll.
With the wind at your back it helps along.
It keeps you on the journey going strong.

And, when, you meet the end of the road.
A friend will be waiting, to bear the load.
As you turn around and start it over again.
It will be there, mystical, whimsical wind.

2021

IN THE AIR

Nothing can compare to a sweet breeze

To a warm, summer's night to a winter's freeze

By one's imagination is there to explore

When, one closes their eyes to open lore's door

And spread your arms like a bird in flight

With its majestic power you feel you just might

Be able to fly up in the air and be so free

The wind on your face and the two skies will be

A warm summer's night a winter's freeze

For, nothing can compare, to this sweet breeze

2022

WHISPERING WIND

It flows through the trees it goes how it please.
This whispering wind a magical journey begins.
No one knows where it goes, it comes and goes.
While it dances with delight each day and night.
Sometimes it blows a kiss sometimes it's a miss.
But it will always blow in, this whispering wind.

2021

BE THERE

Wherever you are,

There you will be!

2023

BE LIKE THE TURTLE

Enter a living space with a cautious face
And be slow to enquire a place with trial
Keep treasures safe within a self's place
So life's shell will tow wherever you go
And wherever you are home is never far

2009

LET LADYBUGS COME

Just lay in the grass
And keep perfectly still
No need hunt for them a task
When they come by their free will

2009

HUMMINGBIRD

Look out your window and you may be able to see.
A miracle is in action, hovering, silently in a breeze.
Its delicate wings dance like a tiny ballerina it twirls.
As it leaps from a flower, within each petal, it swirls.
And it gathers nectar from a beak mighty as a sword.
So look out, your window and you may see a reward.

2022

BE NOW

Be in the now
Live your life in the present
When looking back somehow
You'll think of the past and miss it

But is the memory alive
Or is it just what you make it
Why not take today and try
And give your best and not fake it

Be in the now
Live your life in the present
When looking ahead somehow
You think the future will mend it

But are your dreams just to be
Playing in your head that way
Or will they be released set free
And not keep you from living today

2011

BE STILL

Be still

Be real

Be true

Be you

Be near

Be here

Be real

Be still

2012

JUST A ROCK'N

When life is at a fast pace,
And it seems you're in a rat race.
Do you need to be in first place?
Then think, slow down to a safe haste,
Take the time to be just a rock'n.

Sit still and clear your mind,
Rock back and forth and you'll find.
Family and friends, they are so kind!
And together they're there to unwind,
Make the time to be just a talk'n.

Cars pass by and they wave at you,
You're on the front porch nothing to do.
But rock back and forth, if they only knew!
At peace with yourself and with those who,
Take the time to be just a honk'n.

When life is at a fast pace,
And it seems you're in a rat race.
Do you need to be in first place?
Then think, slow down to a safe haste,
Make the time to be just a rock'n.

2011

TAKE IT EASY

It's as simple as apple pie
Just slow down to realize
Life's too short to go fast
A slower pace, it will last

Time keeps going, no end
It is on you, how to spend
Days in a rush and uneasy
Or in peace, taking it easy

2023

LIFE IS A HOOT

Live life like a bird,
For life's a glorious word,
And let your worries go free,
Whatever they may be,
Live a simple life,
Less stress less strife,
So smile and sing to suit,
Life is a hoot!

2012

LIFE WILL BE

Life will be

Let myself free

And fly at will

Worries, be still

Spread my wings

Living will sing

Let myself free

Life will be

2012

BREEZE ON BY

Life is too short, not to take it all in.
Take a deep breath and let life begin.
What exactly is it that you wish to do.
Start making a list and cross it off too.

Don't have regrets celebrate each day.
There's no excuse, so make your way.
This is your chance to live, if you try.
A life is too short it will breeze on by.

2022

JUMP

Close your eyes and imagine you have wings.
I know, it sounds, silly, what this may bring.
But just do it and envision this world beyond.
A world of no boundaries its worries are gone.
By taking the plunge you're becoming so free.
And leaving behind, all you do not need to be.
With the wind in your hair this fall is to dump.
Your yesterdays are forgotten if you just jump.

2021

TAKE A CHANCE

Let the dice roll
Let the chips fall
One must pay life's toll
To climb victory's wall
So roll the dice
So all chips fall
It's not planning advice
In life that matters at all

2007

BEYOND THE SIDEWALK

Where the sidewalk ends
There life will begin
For adventures are found
When you step down
So one must take that step
And then not regret
Because life begins when
The sidewalk ends

2012

CHERISH CHILDHOOD

Cherish childhood,

As youth stood,

And life will send,

Dreams to begin!

2021

PETER PAN PHILOSOPHY

I do believe James Barrie
In open windows

I do believe in Peter
In ageless shadows

I do believe in Wendy
In a mother sings

I do believe in fairies
In dust and wings

I do believe in lost boys
In the good within

I do believe in pirates
In one's evil sin

I do believe in Indians
In the wind knows

I do believe James Barrie
In open windows

2005

JUST A DREAM

Reality

Or surreal

Imaginary

Or for real

For it seems to be

Just a dream

This living thing

Life brings

2011

LULLABY SEA

Within a deep sleep one will float into the sea.
Into the sea a day will end and the night to be.
And one's dreams will be the sail on this ship.
When, one closes their eyes will begin this trip.

With a wink of an eye one prepares to aboard.
As hands will discover a night's yawn, reward.
And soon to begin is this vision in one's head.
To be on this voyage one must be in their bed.

With a blink of an eye the vessel is on its way.
Thru a wave of tears and twinkling stars obey.
And guide one through this journey the night.
It keeps one safe in the dark until the daylight.

With a nod of one's head one has made it thru.
As one sails through the night beyond the blue.
For the day's forgotten and all worries set free.
When, one closes their eyes on the Lullaby Sea.

2009

TAKE ME BACK

Take me back to my younger years.
When, I'd lie in grass and just steer.
My thoughts and visions up so high.
As I watch a shooting star flying by.

Take me back to my dreams of new.
When out a window daydreams flew.
My future goals, I was able to reach.
As I stared not hearing them, preach.

Take me back to days of yesteryear.
When, I'd play hours without a fear.
My only wish was fly high in the air.
As I live a young life, without a care.

2022

CHILDHOOD DAYS

Remember when days were filled with fun
The morning to arise by adventures begun
Friends gather and quarrel at games played
Even one out voted meant everyone stayed

Remember when a creek is there to explore
By the flowing of ice cold water to its shore
And wade through the rocks under our feet
Catch by a minnow or a crawdaddy's defeat

Remember when nights meant time to hide
Flashlights resemble fireflies in seek to find
For bedtime belies a child's end for the day
Dreams to continue children's gift of replay

Remember when days would last for years
And monsters in closets make believe fears
To live in each moment is childhood ways
With the art of play during childhood days

2004

HALCYON DAYS
(Nostalgic Ways)

Bare feet scamper out the back door.
So toes, like little piglets can play in the grass.
And one runs through field of clover.
Do remember the days, happier times in the past.

And fly with a net to catch a butterfly.
With each swish of the hand, a question is asked.
When it, lands on a finger and not fly.
Do remember the days, happier times in the past.

One wades, knee-deep, a nearby pond.
And like an acrobat glides in air to make a splash.
A circus is in mind, a future beyond.
Do remember the days, happier times in the past.

And climb a vast tree to reach the stars.
Imagination controls a spaceship that won't crash.
Hold tight to reach the top one goes far.
Do remember the days, happier times in the past.

Bare feet scamper out the back door.
So toes, like little piglets can play in the grass.
And one runs through field of clover.
Do remember the days, happier times in the past.

2009

GO BEYOND

The path in life doesn't end, there.
Where the sidewalk ends is a dare.
Take that step and discover a new.
There is so much ahead, look into.
One's dreams its day will be gone.
When hesitating not going beyond.

2023

MY HAPPY PLACE

My favorite place
Is my, smile
My happy face!

So in its place
My sadness awhile
Will be erased.

My favorite place
Is my, smile
My happy face!

2012

NOTHING COMPARES

Nothing compares to a smile on your face.
Nothing compares to a friend you embrace.

Nothing compares to the warmth of the sun.
Nothing compares to a song you sing along.

Nothing compares to a snowy winter's walk.
Nothing compares to the time just for a talk.

Nothing compares to the beauty of life anew.
Nothing compares to the love I have for you.

2023

THE BEST DAY

The sun shines on my face
All my troubles are erased
With a blue sky I do eye
A butterfly and bird fly by
There's a skip to my walk
A cheerful smile as I talk
For life is happy and clever
When, it's the best day ever

2012

SO PEACEFUL

It doesn't take much to be in that special place.
Just walk thru nature and one's worries erased.
And instead are melodies, calm the savage soul.
If you decide leave it behind and to take a stroll.
Where, the world is no longer a hustle or bustle.
But a tranquil forest where in life is so peaceful.

2022

PEACEFUL PLACES

Peaceful places
Are friendly faces
Those quiet days
Be replayed
Sit and ponder
And go be yonder
By looking back
When relaxed
Summer flies by
Like the sky
The clouds above
Are pictures of
And with the night
You point in sight
At the stars
By gazing far
Then winter sings
For it can bring
Snow falling down
An angel found
And white on your face
Will be no trace
Of stress around
When lying down
So sit and rock
For thoughts have brought
You together again
Now and then
And live from there
Without a care
One's weathered face
A peaceful place

2011

MY PERFECT PLACE

My perfect place
I just close my eyes
And sit and ponder
And dream and wonder
What I can only realize
Is a perfect place
Away from fear
Away from mere
Hatred I want erased
From all that I see
People crying
People dying
If you don't believe
In one's truth
But what about mine
But I have a mind
To determine a ruse
So I just close my eyes
And sit and ponder
And dream and wonder
What I can only realize
Is a perfect place
Away from here
Away from mere
Civilization displaced
When I'm up in a tree
High up on a branch
High up not a chance
Anybody can find me
My perfect place

2022

KALEIDOSCOPE

Colors of life to see
Surround me
Take a peek
Within its sphere
Tum the world around
And around
Magical images
Do appear
Dancing
Colors of life
Come alive
Transforming
Digits of trees
Summer's leaves
Snowflakes
Winter's sneeze
Icicles
Bicycles
Different shapes
Life makes
Whimsical hues
Imagination's clue
Red and orange
Blue, green
Take a peek
Colors of life to see
Surround me

2009

BE THE BALLOON

I'll close my eyes and think to be.
It comes to mind makes me happy.
And it's not so expensive for cost.
If by chance it flies away gets lost.
But the joy you feel, it's very real.
It floats above without a care near.
And it waves goodbye ones below.
As if to say, to follow me, let's go.
Where the wind blows is its course.
For only the wind knows of course.
The end of the road is not so soon.
Close your eyes and be the balloon.

2022

LET GO

It's a beautiful day to take a stroll.
Out in the fresh air you're able to roll.

And experience how it feels to be alive.
When out in the open just living life.

So take a deep breath, let worries fly.
Not a care in the world, give it a try.

2022

GO WITH THE FLOW

Swim with the current
It's good advice to know
Going against it is a deterrent
When there's strife's undertow

While floating on your back
All those worries will go
Life's too short so relax
And just go with the flow

2012

JUST FLOAT

When life is a river taking you down
And its current takes over, making you drown
Know there is hope to hear one's peaceful sound
By rolling on your back and just float, I have found

2005

LET IT GO

Oh with too much debt more bills is frightful,
But a credit card is so delightful,
And since we owe seems to just grow,
Let It Go! Let It Go! Let It Go!

There's not enough time for shopping,
And the list it still not stopping,
With this and all you need to know,
Let It Go! Let It Go! Let It Go!

When we finally get to sleep tonight,
How I'll hate waking up to an alarm,
But if you really love me right,
You'll get up and I can stay warm.

Oh the kids are awake and they are crying,
And my dear we're still here lying,
But at long as you love Ho, Ho, Ho,
Let It Go! Let It Go! Let It Go!

2011

WHATEVER

When life doesn't go your way,
And nothing seems to matter anyway,
Just go with the flow, you'll feel better,
And say, whatever, whatever, whatever!

When the more you do the less gets done,
And the more you try pleases no one,
Just take a break will make things better,
And say, whatever, whatever, whatever!

When plans have been made for the day,
And for some reason they've been delayed,
Just make the change and it might be better,
And say, whatever, whatever, whatever!

When life doesn't go your way,
And nothing seems to matter anyway,
Just go with the flow, you'll feel better,
And say, whatever, whatever, whatever!

2012

LONG GONE

Long gone are the days of having fun.
When, childhood is over adults begun.
Daydreams forgotten are now the past.
Hard work the order your mold is cast.

Long gone are the days being carefree.
When being your self was you and me.
Daydreams replaced, by nothing there.
Hard work takes over your empty stare.

2023

HARD KNOCKS

Of all, the schools, one should attend.

There is one in life that will never end.

It starts the day of your birth to the last.

For the lessons learned are from its task.

So its teacher not always fair is mocked.

And why life is a school of hard knocks.

2023

FUNDAMENTAL

Eyes wide open, questions spoken, yearning to learn
Pencils writing, lessons reciting, taking turns
Students reading, minds retrieving, every word
Full of wonder, when you're younger, like a bird

Imagination's soaring, when exploring, crossing the bridge
Kindergarten's over, 1st grade is older, just a smidge
And 5th grade today is harder but also play, and knowledge
Elementary is the tool, there's middle school, high school and college

2017

ACTUAL FACTUAL

It is common sense to base things on facts
How one feels is not an argument, it lacks
The ability to prove in one's point of view
Without facts it is like they have not a clue
Don't be fooled by emotions, when, actual
It's trying to do math and not being factual

2023

THE CLOUD

We live under a shadow of communication.
Every step we take is monitored domination.
Within our universe no one is safe to explore.
Go off the grid they'll knock down your door.
So I wear an aluminum foil headdress shroud.
And not constantly watched by an alien cloud.

2020

CHOOSE WISELY

The choices made today,
Will pave your future's way!

2011

LIFE IS MESSY

The alarm goes off at six a.m.
Rise and shine the day begins.
Then coffee starts your engine.
You face the world once again.

Hurry, scurry, their bus is here.
No time for breakfast, "Oh dear."
And late for work again you fear.
Your schedule did not come near.

At the office the boss just smiles.
It's ammunition to be put in a file.
You work for two so stay a while.
This memo says go the extra mile.

Sam's in soccer and Sue in dance.
Dinner is take-out again by chance.
Another school project, not again.
Staying up late to finish it, when.

The alarm goes off at six a.m.
Rise and shine the day begins.
Then coffee starts your engine.
You face the world once again.

2011

FRIENDLY FIRE

When, one is not looking and being at ease
And thinking the danger is far one believes
For the enemy within is as silent as it is sly
It lays dormant, concealed and stays nearby
As it waits and debates the right time attack
Self-image is low so there's no turning back
With words to harm a battle of self will begin
Discharge of bullets hateful destruction within
The fatal blow to oneself will be from this dire
When, danger is not far but from friendly fire

2007

DECEPTION

Mark my word

Secrets unheard

Do not stay hidden

Even the forbidden

Lies of deception

A life's reflection

In time one purpose

Come to the surface

2006

WHAT THE

                What the heck is going on?

All I see is going wrong.

                Doesn't anyone care anymore?

Or is it just a game to keep score.

                Nothing matters, right or wrong.

Make sure you win so rules are gone.

                In its quake are those unaware.

But sadly we're the ones who do not care.

                2012

A SILENT VOICE

Listen within and you may hear

Right from wrong and what to fear

2023

DUPLICITY

Don't be fooled by a pretty face.

Underneath the skin is beauty erased.

And one's true nature is revealed.

Lies of corruption can't be concealed.

For, it is like a mirror's reflection.

When, we believe its cry of deception.

2023

EVENTUALLY

All is Fell
All is Hell
All is Jell
All is Well

2005

RIDE THE STORM

Take the reins of strife on the horse called life.
Get back in the saddle for each time is a battle.
Determination the suit and spurs on your boots.
As you ride the storm being life's earthly form.

2023

BULLY ADVICE

Take life by the horns and just ride it.

Cause one can never just hide from it.

2008

THE BLIND HORSE

I wish to follow the blind horse.
He knows the way and stays on course.
No need for blinders to keep him right.
His trot is steady without his sight.
So I'll keep loading the cart at his back.
As my worries are heavy but he's on track.
And keep me safe to where I want to be.
When, I follow the horse that cannot see.

2012

BEING THERE

Just because you're there doesn't mean you're there.
When, you're on your phone and not showing a care.
You may be with a crowd but in reality you're alone.
With an electronic device that doesn't care it is stone.
It's turning you into a zombie with feelings of a gnat.
And the only way to wake from the dead is to combat.
Your addiction from this thing is a warning to beware.
So put down your phone and live by truly being there.

2023

SALTY ADVICE

Don't rue the day.

But, rule the day!

2006

RAMBLING ROAD

Let's get off the beaten track in life.
Stop following the highway of strife.
Its rigid concrete is beneath your feet.
When grass should be what we greet.
And the trees are the buildings found.
As the sky is an open window around.
So let's discover a new path unknown.
And, follow your own, rambling road.

2022

WAYWARD ONE

Life is a journey on the ocean of time.
We set sail by the wind of days to find.
A destination, its course takes us along.
Maps to follow, but some don't belong.

To float without a care, worries set free.
No need to follow all others life is to be.
Not on a restricted course it's to become.
Be true to yourself being a wayward one.

2023

OFF THE BEATEN TRACK

I look up to the sky, with a wondering eye,
And ponder with why, why do we die.

It's not very clear, what I'm doing here,
When, death seems so near, with all of its fear.

But life is meant to be, a lesson we agree,
Not to be deceived, but to be free.

Free from fear within, free from death when,
It keeps you down in, the hellish state of grim.

So when worries weigh, I'm able to convey,
I'll stare them down and say, out of my way.

2020

WHAT MAY BE

In the scheme of things tomorrow may be for not.
Who knows what it will bring no one knows a lot.
For one's future is a secret until a new day begins.
And there is no guarantee of outcome until it ends.
Why fret, when there is nothing one can really see.
Because nothing in life for certain to what may be.

2023

WATCH OUT

If you're not keeping a watchful eye,
Your life will then sneak by.

2006

PASSING BY

As I am passing by
I looked upon my life, what I have tried
What I will do, a view upon my life
As I am passing by
For life goes by so quickly, so quickly
With not enough time to touch, taste and see
I looked upon a view of my life
As I am passing by
I looked beyond to my death, without breath
By transformation, to a view beyond my death
As I am passing by
For death comes by so quickly, so quickly
With not enough time to touch, taste and see
I looked beyond to a view of my death
As I am passing by

2004

SHOOTING STAR

Life is a journey, on the path of a star.
Our birth is a beginning to go very far.
We shine at night, as the future is new.
With our light, we live, without a clue.

Someday the light will no longer shine.
In death will be our end when it's time.
Live every moment your dreams go far.
Our life is a journey like a shooting star.

2023

QUASAR

Be like a star
Emitting large amounts of energy
Pulsating a star like image
In the telescope of life

Be exceptional
A remote celestial evanesce body
With the ability to engulf
Forces of the universe

Be the evolution
Not afraid to change who you are
This massive black hole
Creator of galaxies

2019

MAGNETAR

High energy, magnetic field
That is what, I want to yield
As a neutron star I wish to be
Radiate God's power thru me

2020

RADIANT

There's an inner glow

In everyone to show

So one must do is begin

Look within and grin

To know how beautiful

You truly are!

2019

RING SHINE

Within oneself one has the power to shine.
Liken to the rings of Saturn,
We are divine.

Our souls are the inner light of the Oculus.
Liken to the power we learn,
A sun is in us.

Follow the path of universal enlightenment.
Liken to the stars this galaxy,
Life is meant.

The creator of the cosmos is power to shine.
Liken to the energy all's seen,
We are divine.

2020

JUST BE

Be just who you are
Be like a shooting star
Be just uniquely you
BE JUST YOU

2011

UNIQUELY YOU

You are unique
Especial as can be
A one of a kind
Like a snowflake

And no one else
Like the stars above
Can then compare
To uniquely you

2010

ODDITIES

What's strange about being strange?
When, no two are alike in this world arranged.
Look around, and what do you see?
Lots of people different because one's oddities.

2023

ROGUE WAYS

Be different, be unique, be the best from the rest.

Be uplifting, be you seek a life's test, do the best.

Be, far reaching not weak, be like an ocean wave.

Be bewitching, not meek so live with rogue ways.

2010

ROAM FREE

Take flight within your mind let your spirit free.
Just make up your mind and let your worries be.
Go out on a limb if taking chances on your own.
No need for permission for a soul wants to roam.
And fly the skies in the eyes of your imagination.
When, exploring new heights with its fascination.

2022

LIVING BREATHING

This thing called life is quite a special gift.
That most of us take for granted.
We simply go thru the day without one lift.
Of a thought or a prayer ranted.

And thank the creator for the creation of life.
We are apart of this cosmic plan.
But we're just a smidge in its universal blithe.
So we must make each day grand.

By living and breathing with a joyful heart.
Knowing the end could be near.
For if we look back, not ahead, a new start.
Our lives will be living so clear.

This thing called life is quite a special gift.
That most of us take for granted.
We simply go thru the day without one lift.
Of a thought or a prayer ranted.

2022

FRAGILE THINGS

I want to touch the fragile things

To feel the joy they will bring

And not be afraid to drop or ding

Life's dear treasures like a king

2010

ABOVE ALL ELSE

Within the body the soul lives.
The breath of life is what it gives.
By one's consciousness to know thy self.
But be gracious to others above all else.

Within our anatomy cells live.
The breath of life is what it gives.
By one's nature to know good health.
But be grateful to others above all else.

Within this universe, mankind lives.
The breath of life is what it gives.
By one's knowledge to know great wealth.
But be generous to others above all else.

2020

MY LIFE MATTERS

As soon as I came to be I was humanity.

As soon as I began to breathe I was free.

As soon as I started to talk I had a voice.

As soon as I tried to walk I had a choice.

As soon as I learned to play I knew how.

As soon as I went to school I know now.

As soon as I grew to me I pray the latter.

As soon as I came to be, my life matters.

2020

WHAT MATTERS

It's the heart that matters

For everything else tatters

So when looks fade away

The heart will always stay

2012

LOVE MATTERS MOST

Look around you and what do you see.

The people of the world just like me.

And you with many colors and shapes.

We are born with and cannot escape.

No one is better, than the other in line.

For, our destiny is the same in time.

There is no reason, for hatred in those.

When, in reality, love matters most.

2020

WHAT MATTERS MOST

Look around you and what do you see.
A world of beauty is beyond these seas.
We live together all Mankind we share.
The earth our home no others compare.
We're in this space from coast to coast.
It is love for others what matters most.

Look around you and what do you see.
A world of beauty is beyond these seas.
We're not alone in this universe shared.
When a place beyond doesn't compare.
Heaven is Father, Son and Holy Ghost.
For their love for us what matters most.

2020

NOTHING ELSE MATTERS

A simple thing as a smile can make all the difference.
By lifting someone's spirit one's happy remembrance.
For life is a collage of memories, good times and bad.
All sunshine will make a desert we're meant to be sad.
So after the storm a radiant rainbow will be one's gift.
A simple thing as a smile has the energy to then uplift.
And believe nothing in this world has power to shatter.
When His love is within you then nothing else matters.

2020

LIVING FOR ME

I have but one life!

Why do I live, others?

I'm constantly worrying.

I'm always giving in.

I never say how I feel.

I try to make them happy.

But, I'm not happy.

I take the time to help out.

But I'm afraid to ask for help.

I wish for them the best.

And settle for myself second best.

I try not to hurt the feelings of others.

Then allow my own feelings to be hurt.

Why do I do this?

I want to start living for me.

And there is nothing wrong,

Or selfish about that!

2011

RECKONING

I reckon,

My life needs,

Checking!

2006

HOLDS WATER

Oh yes, Mr. Rogers, you can go down the drain.
For life like a bathtub is filled with one's wishes.
Only, the plug is pulled going down to the fishes.
You're lost in a cyclone, someone else the blame.

2006

REVISED

One cannot change the past again.

But, one's opportunity can now begin.

2006

HOLDS MORE WATER

You're right, Mr. Rodgers, "You can never go down the drain."
For one's life is like a bathtub and is filled with your wishes.
But one must go with the flow, learn to swim with the fishes.
Life can only take you down, if you let it, yourself the blame.

2006

RIDDANCE

One's deliverance

From fear's interference

A good riddance

2006

TRUTH BE TOLD

Always here
Never fear
Always near
Never seer

Always might
Never fright
Always bright
Never blight

Always aim
Never blame
Always claim
Never shame

Always brave
Never grave
Always behave
Never knave

Always grateful
Never hateful
Always thankful
Never wasteful

Always home
Never roam
Always known
Never alone

2020

SOMETHING ELSE

Something in youth makes me old
Something in antiquity makes me young
Something in tumult gives me peace
Something in peace gives me turmoil
Something in a lie is the truth
Something in truth is an inner lie
Something in justice defends vengeance
Something in vengeance rules justice
Something deep in society is individualism
Something deep in an individual is a society
Something that is not apart of
Something was never something
Something is the being of contrast

1974

GRAYISH

Live life in shades of gray

In shades of gray is one way

Naught to walk thru life in a straight line

Inbetween black and white is not a crime

2007

SHADES OF GRAYS

They come to succumb, our deepest fear
These humanoid shapes that are near
For their physical traits one will not forget
Becomes an uninvited guest one will regret
A head proportionally large and pear-shaped
With almond, opaque, black eyes that gape
Enlarged and rounded posterior skull
That, vary in coloration dark grey to light grey, dull
No visible skeletal structure is noticeably within
Only a tiny and thin torso with tough, smooth skin
Two small nasal openings with no sight of outer ears
Just a horizontal, slit mouth without lips here
Their arms and hands have a long and slender reach
But they lack opposable thumbs and also no teeth
Fingers and toes are like webbed suction cups
With surprising physical strength to pick things up
They have no obvious external sex organs to see
But some have engaged in sexual practices we believe
Sometimes they respond to spiritual beliefs of humans
Usually they're emotionless, calculating and cold among us
They communicate telepathically but can also make sounds
Reports of high pitch clicks, buzzing and beeps when around
They disguise their appearance and alter our surroundings
And there's a sense of missing time around these things
They induce paralysis to mark us and animals so innocent
And inflict pain by injecting fluids using medical instruments
They, may cause illness associated from the radiation of UFO'S
With a fog or haze ambience so when they come no one knows
But they come to succumb, our deepest fear
These humanoid shapes that are near
For their physical traits one will not forget
Becomes an uninvited guest one will regret

2018

LOCH NESS GUESS

From ancient times of Scottish lore
A creature is told, from long before
The written word, on paper and pen
But it's depict, stone carved by men

The mysterious entity first is known
In an account by St. Columba shown
For it did appear a biography written
By an account a swimmer was bitten

Another attack was soon to be made
St. Columba ordered a beast to obey
"Go back" he said, the monster fled
And because of this, the story's led

To many sightings of a Nessie today
It is a dragon, sea serpent some say
Or a plesiosaur dinosaur, at its best
The Loch Ness monster just a guess

2022

BALLAD OF BIGFOOT

A legend of old is told beyond recorded history in time.
And is known by many titles around the world they find.
The common name Sasquatch is from the native Indians.
But there are countless labels given, where do you begin.
Hairy man's been stalking the mountainous woods there.
As large creatures much like a man but with an ape stare.
And they have special powers with the strength of giants.
With characteristics of stealth, for they are noncompliant.
The only evidence of this eight foot beast is its footprints.
Or sightings of tree structures and nests built its imprints.
They'll also holler that puts a cold chill down your spine.
An eerie noise lets you know you're not alone to remind.
There're stories that are told the legend of Bigfoot known.
Who secretly lives in the world only wants to be left alone.

2023

MYSTICAL BIGFOOT

It's no wonder they hide from sight.
For, we would cause harmful blight.
And in the name of science, explain.
Why we dissect and cause them pain.
To discover, how they've evaded us.
So you think our actions they'd trust.
The forest was their home before us.
Stop trying luring them out for a fuss.
Let them alone and be at peace there.
This mystical Bigfoot, show we care.

2022

NOBODY CARES

I'm not afraid of death
But of dying to my last breath

I'm not afraid of others around
But being alone in a crowd

I'm not afraid of different opinions
But a silence of words division

I'm not afraid of weather changing
But of solar flares rearranging

I'm not afraid of a carbon gas breeze
But the lack of trees to breathe

I'm not afraid of Sasquatch
But feeling you're being watched

I'm not afraid of a UFO persuasion
But of an alien race invasion

I'm not afraid of galaxies colliding
But our planet earth abiding

I'm not afraid of an afterlife
But not knowing if it's joy or strife

I'm not afraid of the Most High
But not asking the question why

I'm not afraid of thoughts I share
But that nobody cares

2022

WITHIN

Within my heart, there is a song written.
With words to express my life's smitten.

Within my mind there are thoughts there.
With memories ingrained I wish to share.

Within my dreams there are eagle wings.
With wishes I will make, they will bring.

Within my convictions there is truth said.
With the hope they stay alive not be dead.

2023

COMING AND GOING

Every minute of the day someone is born.
For, a baby cries with each new morn.
When angels at birth, so sweet and innocent.
They renew life on earth, they're heaven sent.

Every minute of the day someone dies.
For, death is there when a loved one cries.
When angels above are heaven sent.
They retrieve life on earth, there souls went.

2012

LET IT JUST BE

When, we die nothing will matter.
For, all our dreams and fears will shatter.
When, death takes us by the hand.
For, the day ends and the night commands.

When, the stars guide us to a place.
For, we travel beyond and time is erased.
When, this world no longer we see.
For, we must let life go, and let it just be.

2020

THE CHANGE

I rose one day and I was not the same
I do not remember when
The change came about

Did I slumber through the days
Believing fate would bend
The rules of life in years' amount

I was but a child was I naught
Yesterdays when I slept
But the days were added on

This will not happen to me I thought
A child I want to be I wept
My years of youth alas gone

Grown I am now
No longer a child in youth
I awoke to this new strife

With the change no warning allowed
A silence is kept to the truth
When entering into adult life

2002

GROWING OLD IS NOT FOR SISSIES

When I look in the mirror, who do I see?

I see someone else in the mirror, not me.

For the person I see has grown very old.

But the person in me is still young and bold.

So how can I feel the way that I feel?

When, it's so hard to get out of bed and deal.

With the aches and pains within my bones.

When I look in the mirror I'm not known.

For once upon a time by morning I was spry.

Now I just sleep because all I want to do is lie.

In my bed is where I want to be.

As my body is weak but my spirit is free.

So when I look in the mirror, who do I see?

I see, growing old is not for sissies!

2012

IMPRISONED IN TIME

In the mirror there is a reflection of an age.
But the mind believes it's not turned a page.
It is imprisoned by memories of one's past.
A breath in time forever stamped, and cast.

2005

SEQUENT

I held your hand being you were so young,
Your miniature fingers disappearing in mine,
I won't let go, a life's walk has begun,
A change lies beside this one moment in time.

For the years come and go, a circlet in time,
Being, it is my hand held, I am not so young,
Your fingers will no longer disappear in mine,
Don't let me go a death's walk has begun.

2005

HOME SWEET HOME

Sold are those possessions accumulated throughout the years
Or maybe scattered among the family for memories held dear
With pictures being displayed on corkboard to show they care
So few of them do bother visiting, with mom out of their hair

A routine is established with one's breakfast, lunch and dinner
It will be the highlight of their day also being the bingo winner
Then wheelchairs are corralled like cattle back into a tiny room
And once again forgot as a caged animal that is seen at the zoo

Life is just waiting and waiting, for what they don't even know
Death is just waiting and waiting with luck they're in line to go
Getting old is not for wimps as it takes true courage to be alone
By living in a nursing facility and told this is home sweet home

2010

BREVITY

With each breath is the shortness of time.
For the countdown has started at our birth.
Our inhaling takes in life's energy sublime.
When, exhaling has us closer leaving earth.

2022

BEYOND THE STARS

Somewhere beyond the stars
Way up I'll go far
There I will feel so free
That is where I want to be

Somewhere beyond the night
Way up in my flight
There I will look below
That is where I want to go

2023

INEVITABLE

Inevitably no matter how hard one tries

In the end, you're not getting out alive!

2020

www.ingramcontent.com/pod-product-compliance
Lightning Source LLC
LaVergne TN
LVHW041709070526
838199LV00045B/1273